The Ninja guide to
FINANCIAL LITERACY
FOR HIGH SCHOOL STUDENTS

Learn the tips you need to know as a high school student today

Cecelia Nowlin

Copyright © 2019

All rights reserved. No part of this book may be reproduced, stored in a retrieval system, or transmitted in any form or by any means, electronic, mechanical, photocopying, recording, scanning, or otherwise, without the prior written permission of the publisher.

Disclaimer

All the material contained in this book is provided for educational and informational purposes only. No responsibility can be taken for any results or outcomes resulting from the use of this material.

While every attempt has been made to provide information that is both accurate and effective, the author does not assume any responsibility for the accuracy or use/misuse of this information.

Dedication

The journey going from a high school student to going into to the real world is not easy. I want to dedicate this book to all the parents who want to give their child the foundation they need.

Table of Contents

CHAPTER 1: Financial Literacy 7
CHAPTER 2: Life Skills as High School Students 11
CHAPTER 3: Consumer Skills 19
CHAPTER 4: Starting Credit as a Student 23
CHAPTER 5: Managing Debts 27
CHAPTER 6: Preparing For Higher Education 31
CHAPTER 7: Insurance Basis as a Student ... 35

CHAPTER 1: Financial Literacy

As high school students, you have to realize you won't be in high school forever; you will eventually graduate from high school into college and soon stop depending on your parents/guardians financially. This is why it is important to learn how to be financially dependent; financial literacy is important when learning to be dependent and when dealing with finances especially for high school students.

What is financial literacy?

Financial literacy is defined as being educated and understanding different financial areas such as managing personal finance, making money and knowing how to invest. However, financial literacy focuses more on the ability of a person to manage their personal finance matters in a very efficient manner. For you to be financial literate, you have to have the knowledge of making certain decisions about your personal finance such as insurance, retirement, tax planning. For high school students, it has to be the case of making financial decisions about paying for college, budgeting, and investment.

The Importance of Financial Education for High School Students

Financial literacy helps high school students become self-sufficient in order to achieve financial stability. What are the behaviors and attitudes high school students possess about money, and how do they apply it to their daily lives? Financial literacy demonstrates this. Financial literacy shows how a student makes financial decisions. Financial education helps a person develop a financial road map to identify how much he/she earns, how he/she spends the earning and what he/she owes. Let me paint a scenario:

Toby earns $300 per month in income. His monthly expenses include his apartment utility bills of about $100. From the remaining $200, he pays $100 for her monthly gym subscription that offers a whole lot of services (which are not entirely utilized by him). He also uses the remaining $100 leftover to buy expensive clothing items in the name of brand clothing. This means that at the end of the month he is left with no saving for any unforeseen circumstances, which he might actually incur.

This is where financial education comes in. Students who are financial literates are more likely to save money successfully, budget wisely and invest smartly.

It is important that we re-evaluate how we are educating students (or not educating students) on the importance of financial literacy.

Contrary to belief, financial illiteracy doesn't affect only older adults; it affects people of all ages and all socioeconomic levels. Lack of financial education causes a lot of people to become victims of fraud, and high-interest rates, which might result in bad credit, bankruptcy or even foreclosure.

Financial illiteracy can lead to a person making really poor financial decisions and owing large amounts of debt. A Financial Industry Regulatory Authority conducted a research, and the results showed that about 60% of Americans are financial illiterates. Reconciling bank accounts, paying bills on time, paying off debt and planning for the future are basic skills that most Americans lack.

In order to bridge the gap between high school and college, Pennsylvania State University has prepared a study program to promote financial literacy and put high school students through making good decisions about their financially well-being.

CHAPTER 2: Life Skills as High School Students

As a high school student, you're not too young to start learning certain life skills. Before a high school student goes to college, it is important that they learn certain life skills that will help them thrive. But some of these core life skills are mostly ignored and neglected.

As a high school student, if you don't have certain life skills you are not only going to be faced with the challenge of being a new college student; but you are also going to have difficulty in managing your adulthood life. However, when you take the time to learn some life skills in advance, you can relieve this burden, and make your transition into your new phase of life so much easier.

Here are some life skills you need to learn as a high school student:

Grocery Shopping And Basic Cooking

This might sound like something really trivial but

cooking is a life skill and a survival skill. Unless the idea of your living off Top Ramen, Pizza Rolls and fast food sounds appealing, it is important that they know how to do grocery shopping and basic cooking. This also helps in saving money as everything you need is right in your kitchen. You do not need to start spending money on expensive fast food.

Vehicle Maintenance And Repair

For high school students who will have a car with them when they eventually get to college, learning how to properly maintain their vehicle and handle basic repairs are life skills that are very important. When you learn the basics of vehicle repair, you can fix the minor problems you might encounter with your vehicle. This would save you time and money.

Money Management

Money management is a very important life skill. Talking about money might not always be comfortable, but it is important that you should understand how to handle the basics such as budgeting and bill payments. These are crucial life skills you should learn as a high schooler before heading to college. This is even more relevant if you have to use student loans to fund a portion of your education or if you are receiving most of your financial support in the form of scholarships, you will have to learn to effectively manage your finances to last you through the semester or year.

Banks

Talking about money management and saving, we all know where it is safe to keep our money; a bank. A bank is a financial institution that is licensed to receive deposits and make loans. Banks are also allowed to provide financial services such as; management of wealth, currency exchange, and safe deposit boxes. There are two major types of banks; commercial banks (also known as retail banks) and investment banks.

Before I go into details on how a high school student can save and invest money, let me shed more light on how banks work.

How do banks work?

Banks work by simply paying their customers to lend them money (sounds a little complicated?). When a person deposits money into their bank account, the bank takes that money and lend other people. The customer that deposited the money gains a small amount of money in return (that is the interest on savings), and the customer that lends money from the bank pays a larger amount of money to the bank in return (that is the interest on loans). In order to make money for themselves, banks keep the bigger difference.

Understand banking can be quite difficult, since banks are very different from other businesses. However, one thing we know is that they are highly leveraged, with more than $30 in debt for every $1 of equity. Since they don't make any real products, it can be hard to understand what banks actually do. Although a large number of people seem to think that banking is "free", this might be because banks keep advertising free checking and savings accounts, free direct deposit, etc.

Banking products

I know I said banks don't make any real products; this doesn't mean they don't make products at all.

Bank products means any bank service offered to the customers, such as: credit cards, credit card processing services, debit cards, purchase cards, ACH transactions, cash management, including controlled disbursement, accounts or services, a checking and saving account.

We are going to focus on checking and savings account.

Although they can be used together, a checking account and saving account are two different accounts.

A checking account is a deposit account opened in banks, it allows withdrawals and deposits. A checking account is also known as a demand account/transactional account. A checking account is very liquid; it is mostly accessed using checks, automated teller machines, and electronic debits. A checking account is different from other bank accounts this is because it allows numerous withdrawals and unlimited deposits. However, savings accounts have a certain limit on both.

A savings account is the most common type of bank account (after a checking account). Savings accounts allow you to keep your money in a safe place while it accumulates small amount of interest every month. A savings account is a reliable way to keep your cash and earn money through interest; this interest is the percentage the bank pays you just for keeping money in the account. The more you save, the more interest you earn each month. (This should be motivation enough for you to save).

Learning about Budgeting

Budgeting is an important part of financial education for a high school student. To become financially dependent, you have to learn to manage and budget your funds.

What is a budget?

Budgeting is the process of drafting a plan to help you spend your money. This spending plan is what is called a

budget. Creating a budget helps you determine whether you have enough money to do the things you need or would like to do.

Budgeting Skills

Budgeting skill is an important skill to learn as a high school student. The ability of a person to manage his/her own money is known as budgeting skills. Budgeting skills involve making conscious decisions about allocating money. Budgeting skill is a great tool for planning and controlling your expenditures as a student.

How to start a budget as a student

To become financially dependent, the first step to take is to create a budget to help manage and spend your money. These are ways you can start a budget as a student:

1. Record your expenses-

Do you notice how fast your cash disappears? You can start a budget by getting a handle on where your cash is going. Get a notebook or use a phone app to record even the smallest expenses such as snacks, movie tickets, etc. Some expenses you don't find relevant enough are often ignore, expenses like music downloads, phone data etc. Record them so they'll be easy to track.

2. Organize your records-

Find a system that is sufficient to use to track and organize your expenses and financial records. There are mobile apps that can help you track your financial information. Make sure you are consistent in doing this.

3. Create a routine-

Create a routine; if you discover that you can't record your expenses every day, record them weekly. Once you begin to wait for than a week to record information, you may forget some expenses and become overwhelmed with the information.

4. Create an 'unforeseen' category in the budget-

Create a category in your budget and tag it as unforeseen budget. This is where you'll save money in to be prepared for unforeseen costs.

CHAPTER 3: Consumer Skills

Consumer skills are the skills individual customers and groups develop to satisfy their needs and wants. It refers to the actions of the consumers in the marketplace and the skills learnt to invoke the action.

Basic Consumer Skills

These are the basic consumer skills every high school student needs to know/acquire:

1. Budgeting- budgeting is a basic consumer skill. It helps you plan ahead on what to buy and priority to set.
2. Bargaining- bargaining is also a necessary basic consumer skill. Negotiating for a price helps reduce your cost and helps you stick to your budget.

Preparing To Buy First Car

As a high schooler soon to graduate, you will be looking forward to buying your first card. You get happy when you realize that you no longer have to rely on public transport. Having a car gives you the privilege of going anywhere you want, at any time.

Before you buy a car, here are a few tips that will help you for preparation:

1. Buy the car you can afford

Sure, you have the image of the latest high-horsepower car model in your mind but you have to realize that you can't afford it. You can buy a car that's affordable now and save up for your dream car later. This will help you not acquire debt.

2. Think about the unforeseen costs

Encountering unforeseen costs is inevitable when you own a car. These costs involve car repairs. You need to budget monthly for these unforeseen costs.

3. Check online reviews

You are advised to go online to see product reviews about the car you want to buy. Reviews often give you valuable on what you want to buy.

4. Inspect the car

Before you purchase a car, have a mechanic do a thorough inspection of the car and test run it. The seller car might be holding back critical information about the car from you. Also, ask for the necessary paperwork just to make sure that the car wasn't stolen.

Preparing To Move Away From Home

Once a high school student is through with high school and is moving the college, there is a 100% chance that they are moving far away from home. As a student this is the first step to financial independence is moving away from your parents/guardian.

You might be having the mixed feelings of nervousness and excitement at the same time. Excited that you finally have freedom, but nervous that you'll be away from family.

Here are some tips to need while preparing to move away from home:

- **Resolve family issues before you leave-**

    Are you still mad at your mom for not attending your drama night? Or mad at your sibling for snitching on you to your parent? If you have an unresolved issue with your parent or siblings, it is best to resolve it before leaving home. Negative feelings can affect the way you will interact with people on campus.

- **Start practicing healthy habit**

  It is known that most students (especially college students) don't practice healthy habits. Most are sleep-depraved and don't eat healthy. You should learn to start practicing healthy habits. Take your

- **Learn how to manage your funds**

  Leaving home is accompanied by financial responsibility. It might be overwhelming at first but once you learn to budget and manage, you'll get the hang of it.

- **Do what you love**

  Once you leave home and get to college, don't forget to keep doing things you love. Where you a cheerleader or a band geek in high school? You can join the campus orchestra. Find a club of what you love doing and join the club.

CHAPTER 4: Starting Credit as a Student

Starting credit is one of the steps you have to take to becoming financially independent as a student. Building good credit is very important. Building credit will help you qualify for loans, cell phone plans, insurance, and even prospects of getting a job. Before we go into how you can build credit as a student;

What is credit?

A credit is an agreement between a borrower and a lender. The borrower borrows something of value and agrees to pay the lender at a particular time, generally with interest.

What is credit score?

A credit score is a number/are numbers used to analysis the credit files of a person, a credit score represents the creditworthiness of a person. Primarily, a credit score is based on a credit report.

Banks and credit card companies (lenders) use credit scores to know if it is risky to lend money to certain consumers. However, credit scoring is not limited to just banks, some organizations, such as landlords, insurance companies and mobile phone companies amongst many others also use credit scoring.

Managing Credit

Managing a credit score of 850 can be extremely rare (once a person with the score of 850 applies for credit, that score drops because of an inquiry). However, you don't need to reach the score of 850 to be perfect. Any score above 750 is considered perfect.

What Affects Your Credit Score

There are certain things/situations that can affect your credit score, here are some of them:

1. Your payment history-

Your payment history determines about 40% of your credit score. How fast and timely you pay your bills can affect your credit score. Severe payment issues, like repossession, bankruptcy, charge-offs and others like these can affect your credit score. The best advice is to make your payments on time each month for a perfect credit score.

2. Debt Levels

Your debt level determines about 25% of your credit score. Credit scoring calculations are also based on some factors relating to your debt. The overall debt you carry can affect your credit score. However, your credit score can improve and become perfect once you pay down your debts.

3. The age history of your credit

How long have you had your oldest credit account? Age of credit determines about 15% of your credit score. Having an older credit age history improves your credit score because this means that you have a lot of experience when it comes to handling credit. When you open new accounts or close the old accounts, there is a chance that this will lower your average credit age. For that reason, it I'd advised that you don't open a lot of new accounts at once.

4. The types of credit you have on your report-

Basically, there are two types of credit accounts, they are revolving accounts and installment loans. It is good to have both types of accounts on your credit report, this improves for your credit score and it also shows that you have experience in managing different types of credit.

Having loans for different types of assets is even

better. Assets such as a car or a house, in addition to credit cards, and a student or personal loan. However, having various types of credit only contributes to 10% of your credit score, so not having a certain type of credit, won't really damage your credit score.

5. The number of credit Inquiries

Every time you submit an application that involves the requirement of a credit check, this shows that you made a credit-based application and an inquiry is placed on your credit report. Inquiries make up only 10% of your credit score. Having about one or two inquiries won't have much effect, but having several inquiries, especially within a short period of time cost you a really low credit score. It is important that you keep your applications to a minimum to preserve your credit score.

The good news is that inquiries made within the last 12 months will affect your credit score but they will completely disappear from your credit report after 24 months.

CHAPTER 5: Managing Debts

What is a debt?

Debt is when something (in most cases money) is owed by one party (the borrower), to another party (the lender). Debt is a payment you defer from paying at that particular time, which is why it is different from an immediate purchase.

As a high school student soon going college the first things that should be on your mind is saving money, managing dents, the use of credit card wisely, and pretty much anything having to do with budgeting or money.

However, if you are not careful college can create a financial future full of debt. A lot of credit card offers in the mail that seem too good to be true will be offered to you, but if you are not careful you would definitely wind up having more debt than just your student loans after you graduate.

Here are some great debt management tips for students:

1. Learn how to budget:

This keeps being reported because it is extremely important. As a student, budgeting is one of the most important tools and basic life skills that you can learn. Learn how to manage your debts by creating a budget. Make sure it is realistic and you can stick with it. Remember, it is better to budget now and live within your means as this will make it easier for you to get out of debt faster once you have graduated and started your career journey.

2. Use of credit cards-

Signing up for credit cards and using them for everyday purchases is one of the biggest temptation of a student, especially a college student. College students are magnets for credit card offers. The credit card lenders know that most college students have a growing present need for money and a financial prospect in the future.

Learning how to control credit card use is good for debt management. As tempting as it may be to use a credit card for different things like shopping, eating out, etc. Curbing almost all credit card purchases is a really good idea. Whatever you are buying will cost way more than the price tag this is because of the interest on credit cards. It easy to acquire unnecessary debt with credit cards. You most likely would have student loans to pay off once you graduate from college adding credit card debt to all of that is really not a good idea.

3. Choosing the right student loan-

Student loans is mostly the common way students pay for college. It is important to choose the right student loan. Student loans are also known as smart debt, this is due to the asset that college gives you (a college degree). Student loans, especially the ones federal government provides usually have decent terms. Since the interest will begin to accumulate immediately you take a student loan, it is advisable to start making payments while still in school. This will help you chip away at the interest.

4. Have emergency savings-

It is advisable to have an emergency fund. You can now avoid the need to put a surprise expense on a credit card. Once you acquire a credit card, keeping the interest paid off every single month is the best way to manage debt, and having an emergency savings fund will make it much easier to handle unforseen and unanticipated costs.

CHAPTER 6: Preparing For Higher Education

As a high school student, graduating from high school and preparing for higher education is important. College is the first step into adulthood, and it determines one's future. Waiting for it can sometimes become an exciting yet nerve-racking experience.

As a high schooler, the questions on your mind would be:

- What is my college of choice and how do I apply?
- Am I good enough to attend this college?
- Will I pass the entrance exams?
- How do I start planning for college?

The truth is that there is no magic portion or formula to make sure you get accepted into the college of your choice. But there are certain factors and tips that can help.

It is important that your college major is something you will enjoy studying. You will do better in school if you like the subjects you are studying. You also may find it easier to explain to potential employers what you gained from school. You can start preparing for college with the tips below:

1. Take the necessary high school courses-

Review a list of recommended high school courses you are taking and make sure they meet the minimum requirements of the college of your choice. Also start reading early on the courses you'll be studying in college.

2. Earn college credits early-

It is possible for you to earn college credit or advanced placement credits while in high school, do a little research on how to can earn college credit. Take advantage of Postsecondary Enrollment Options (PSEO).

3. Learn some self-assessment skills-

Self- assessment helps you learn about your strengths, skills and interests. Write a list of your interest and skills, this should give you an insight on what to major in.

4. Research majors and type of degrees-

Create a list of types of majors and degrees that interests you. Then use that list to pick the schools and programs of your choice.

5. Take part in extracurricular activities-

Students who actively participates in extracurricular activities while planning for college are valued by colleges. Therefore, it is important to find and engage in an activity that interests you. A good option is to apply for pre-college summer programs.

6. Apply for internship programs-

This step is optional but once you get an opportunity to do it, it can be very helpful. Internships helps us kick start our career paths so it is important that you apply for one, if you can.

7. Develop your writing skills-

If you are someone who doesn't like writing, you have to develop it for college purposes. You can do research using some term papers, libraries and proper internet resources can also help you with research. Once your writing and researching skills are really developed, you are guaranteed to get an A.

8. Develop time management skills-

Learn how to manage your time, your classes would be on schedule, so getting up early and getting to classes on time is important. You can create a schedule on your phone or computer, where you record how you are using your time. Also make out a study time, for example, 30-40 minutes in a day or more.

9. Develop speaking skills-

Speaking up in class might be something you're not comfortable with, but in college you'll have to make a presentation in front of a whole class. You can start by making notes about what you want to say before speaking so that you get prepared.

10. Prepare early for exams-

Start preparing early for college entrance exams. Try to find out if the college you are applying for requires the ACT or the SAT exams. Study and take pre-tests that focuses on the area you're weak at.

CHAPTER 7: Insurance Basis as a Student

What is life insurance?

Life insurance (also called life assurance, mostly in the Commonwealth of Nations) is a contract an insurer/assurer and an insurance policy, where the insurer is to pay a beneficiary a sum of money (the benefit) in exchange for a premium, upon the death of the person who got insured (most times it is the policy holder). Depending on the type of contract, other events such as critical or terminal illness can also trigger payment. Expenses like funeral benefits are also included in the benefits.

As a college student, the last thing on your mind is life insurance. You are more focused on passing your grades and preparing for your future career. However, seeking out life insurance as a college student will give you and your family some peace of mind in case any accident or unforeseen health problem arises. Thinking about it might be unpleasant, but it is better to be safe than sorry especially when it comes to preparing for the future.

There are some reasons why college students need life insurance.

1. For life insurance purposes-

This is the primary reason everyone needs life insurance, you never know what is going to happen. A lot of people think that young people don't need life insurance, which is very untrue. A good life insurance policy will expenses your family may incur because of your death and cover funeral expenses.

2. Coverage of outstanding debts-

Life insurance can cover any outstanding debts that a student has after their death. We all know that college is very expensive, and a lot of students take out loans to cover their education. Once you take out federal student loans, in the event of your death, the rest of the debt will be cancelled. However, once you opt for private student loans, you'll still have to pay off your debts regardless of the situation. Asides from student loans, many parents use other borrowing methods to pay for their children's education, this would also still need to be repaid regardless. A competent life insurance policy will cover the amount of money that a student owes in the event of their unlikely death, whether it is a student loan or not.

As a student who has dependents, it is very important to take out a life insurance policy, even if you are healthy.

Buying Life Insurance As A College Student

When buying life insurance as a college student, there are certain things you need to consider. College is already expensive, so it is very important that find a life insurance policy that will not disrupt your budget. Most times, it is actually better to go with a term life insurance policy. Term life insurance policies are set for a certain period of time, you can also choose to renew or cancel that insurance when that time period is up. Another benefit is that they are much more affordable than whole life insurance policies and can easily fit into a college student's budget. A very good benefit of a term life insurance plan is that you do not have to renew your insurance plan once college is over. After you finish college, your loans and debts are taken care of, if you don't feel like you need it anymore, you can cancel or change the terms.

Even though you want an insurance plan that fits into your budget, you should also make sure you have enough coverage for insurance. Take a paper and add up the amount of your student loans and any other financial debts your family would owe in the event of your death. You will need to take out at least the money you added up for your life insurance policy. You should also take out more than your loan amounts, just so that your family will have enough money for the funeral expenses.

Before you sign anything, make sure you read the fine print of the life insurance policy document to make sure it actually covers the loan repayment you are going to need in the future. Note that every insurance policy is different, and you need to make sure yours is suitable for your needs. Work with an insurance company that you trust, meet up and have a discussion with an insurance professional before you finalize anything.

www.ingramcontent.com/pod-product-compliance
Lightning Source LLC
Chambersburg PA
CBHW070844220526
45466CB00002B/879